Faith
Dilemmas
for
Marketplace
Christians

Faith Dilemmas for Marketplace Christians

A resource for small groups

**Ben Sprunger,
Carol J. Suter,
& Wally Kroeker**

Herald
Press

*Scottdale, Pennsylvania
Waterloo, Ontario*

Library of Congress Cataloging-in-Publication Data
Sprunger, Ben, 1937-
    Faith dilemmas for marketplace Christians : a resource for small
groups / Ben Sprunger, Carol J. Suter, and Wally Kroeker.
        p. cm.
    ISBN 0-8361-9074-2 (alk. paper)
    1. Christian ethics. 2. Business ethics. I. Suter, Carol J., 1949-
II. Kroeker, Wally, 1946- . III. Title.
BJ1275.S67 1997
241'.64—dc21   97-23652

The paper used in this publication is recycled and meets the minimum
requirements of American National Standard for Information Sciences
—Permanence of Paper for Printed Library Materials, ANSI
Z39.48–1984.

All Bible quotations are used by permission, all rights reserved, and
unless otherwise indicated are from the *New Revised Standard Version
Bible,* copyright 1989, by the Division of Christian Education of the
National Council of the Churches of Christ in the USA. NIV quotes are
from *The Holy Bible, New International Version*, copyright © 1973,
1978, 1984 International Bible Society, Zondervan Bible Publishers.

FAITH DILEMMAS FOR MARKETPLACE CHRISTIANS
Copyright © 1997 by Herald Press, Scottdale, Pa. 15683
    Published simultaneously in Canada by Herald Press,
    Waterloo, Ont. N2L 6H7. All rights reserved
Library of Congress Catalog Number: 97-23652
International Standard Book Number: 0-8361-9074-2
Printed in the United States of America
Book and cover design by Gwen M. Stamm

06 05 04 03 02 01 00 99 98 97 10 9 8 7 6 5 4 3 2 1

Contents

Preface

Each day we start our faith journey anew. New dilemmas come our way. They require us to face hard and unclear choices. Often we must act without specific scriptural direction or common understanding among those with whom we worship. This book explores how we or members of our family and church might handle such situations.

At work our colleagues, bosses, employees, customers, and suppliers observe our conduct. Hardly a day goes by when our faith and actions do not intersect. A survey of 2,000 administrative assistants and secretaries reveals an "alarming frequency of ethical misbehavior in the business office today," says office ethics expert Nan DeMars. As the old saying goes, our actions may speak louder than our words. How then do others view our actions? How does our faith temper our actions?

As president of Mennonite Economic Development ment Associates (MEDA), I am privileged to work with businesspeople who earnestly desire to integrate their Christian faith with their lives in the marketplace. From them and others in the church, I hear questions like these: How can we shorten the distance between what we hear on Sunday and what we face on Monday? How can we discuss our workplace conflicts in a church setting? How can we give one another the support and counsel we need to be faithful disciples in our daily work?

We decided to assemble a number of actual workplace dilemmas into a handy format for small-group discussion. I was assisted by Carol Suter, an attorney and our vice-president of Member and Resource Development, and by Wally Kroeker, editor of our magazine, *The Marketplace*. Both of them, by virtue of their roles within MEDA, regularly deal with the interplay of faith and work.

The result of our efforts is this book. It looks at thirteen workplace situations and asks how persons of faith might respond. The studies emerge out of actual experiences, although we have altered some facts to preserve confidentiality.

Why did we choose case studies? First, when examining dilemmas, it is usually less threatening to observe what others experience. Dilemmas are situations where the right answer or appropriate action is not readily apparent. For the Christian, dilemmas are often dilemmas precisely because specific scriptural imperatives are missing. You will quickly note that, as in life, the book does not give answers. You are invited to find answers using critical as well as reflective thinking in conversation with others. With case studies, you can safely test and rethink what your response or actions might be.

Second, case studies allow us to live vicariously in the shoes of another. Whether studying these alone or in vigorous discussion with others, you can for a few moments live another's situation. For example, even if you are not a business owner, you can still experience the dilemma of Menno and Vera Wenger as found in case study one. In case study six, you can feel for Warren, who is being pressured to produce more when suddenly an opportunity—though a questionable one—arises. You can test with others what it means to be a person of faith in the workplace. If we walk in another's shoes, it may help us to be more understanding and less judgmental as others also attempt to be faithful to Christ in difficult circumstances.

Since we are to be Jesus' disciples, we are also called to go into all the world and preach the gospel. Not all of us are called specifically to church work or active mission work. Yet each day others watch us and draw conclusions about our character and what we hold to be truth. We can learn from each other's experiences, insights, and challenges. We trust this book will help us grow in understanding of what it means to follow Christ in daily life and in the marketplace.

—Ben Sprunger, President,
Mennonite Economic Development Associates
(MEDA)

Faith
Dilemmas
for
Marketplace
Christians

1 Feeling Guilty About Expansion

See, I have chosen Bezalel, . . . and I have filled him with the Spirit of God, with skill, ability and knowledge in all kinds of crafts —to make artistic designs for work in gold, silver and bronze, to cut and set stones, to work in wood, and to engage in all kinds of craftsmanship.

—Exodus 31:2-5, NIV

A WOMAN, asked about her family, said, "I have two grown children. One is in business; the other is serving the Lord."

Those who work at "secular" jobs, whether in business or other professions, are not always seen as active Christian servants. Some are even regarded as second-class citizens in the kingdom of God.

Not all of us are gifted to be pastors or missionaries. Nonetheless, we too have been given occupational assignments through which we can be God's junior partners in meeting the daily needs that help sustain

God's creation. Scripture suggests that our daily work is a calling through which we can exercise the gifts God has given us.

*   *   *

It was a quiet Saturday evening. Menno and Vera Wenger were relaxing in their favorite chairs after an active week in the business they jointly owned and operated. Menno pondered the financial reports he'd just read. They gave him a sense of both joy and dread.

Profits were up. Menno was grateful for a good year, for their thriving company, for their twenty-two employees. On the other hand, he felt unease because ticklish decisions lay ahead.

Last year profits had been small, leaving few things to decide. They merely increased wages where they could. What little surplus was left went to up-grade equipment and hire two new employees. Menno and Vera's personal income had been only slightly above average for people in the area.

Menno wouldn't forget the last time profits had been this good. They had added a production line, hired seven more people, and built a much-needed warehouse. It was a handsome building, conspicuous from the main road. Its visible location gave customers easy access and projected a dynamic image.

That, unfortunately, had been the problem, at least for people quick to criticize. Menno and Vera felt the sting of comments, only half-humorous, that they were building a monument to themselves. Someone joked that it housed an indoor golf course. Another muttered about "a license to steal." That hurt.

Menno almost wished this year had been like the last. He didn't relish making choices that would bring more sarcasm.

People didn't understand how vulnerable the company was. They didn't realize that running a business meant being in a permanent relationship with the bank and having to worry constantly about the prime rate. Things were going well now, but the market was unpredictable. To stay competitive in a changing environment, they needed more trucks, a bigger building, and at least seven or eight more workers.

That last part felt good. It was fulfilling to Menno and Vera that their vision and hard work created good jobs at competitive wages. Their employees meanwhile were building their own capital base. Out of it they sustained their families, paid for houses, helped finance schools, and generally contributed to the community. When the Wengers created new jobs, they almost felt as if they were doing the Lord's work, though they wouldn't describe it that way at church.

Ah yes, church. Tomorrow was Sunday. Menno and Vera would encounter some employees and their families. Would the Wengers' looming decisions interfere with their worship? What would be the mood of the service and the sermon topic? Would they feel joyous or guilty?

Questions to ponder and discuss

1. To whom in the church can the Wengers go for counsel and sharing? What can be done to create a safe environment? Is the church the place for this kind of sharing?

2. How should the Wengers balance priorities? Should they expand the business? Give more in wages, bonuses, and benefits? Give more to the church and charities? What Scripture would be helpful?

3. Let's say you're the pastor of a church which includes people like the Wengers as well as others who don't understand the Wengers' dilemma. How would you plan next Sunday's service and message? How would you bridge different viewpoints?

Additional Scripture

See also Matthew 25:14-28; Luke 12:48;
1 Corinthians 4:2; Colossians 3:17; 1 Peter 4:10.

2 Time to Share?

*Always be prepared to give an answer to every-
one who asks you to give the reason for the hope
that you have. But do this with gentleness and
respect. . . .*

—1 Peter 3:15-16, NIV

OVERZEALOUS Christians who ignore Pe-
ter's words on "gentleness and respect" have given
witnessing a bad name.

Others have overreacted by muting their verbal
witness entirely. Writer Patrick Klingaman confesses
that he, like many other Christians, is usually eager to
share his political opinions but tends to take a vow of
silence when it comes to sharing opinions about Jesus Christ. Perhaps it is time to remind ourselves of
the old saying, "When the heart is on fire, sparks will
fly out of the mouth."

*   *   *

Ian had the problems of Job, but so far his work hadn't suffered. Though sometimes frazzled, he still completed his projects on time and on target. On the surface everything seemed fine with Doreen's star employee.

However, it wasn't. From a reliable source, she learned that Ian's personal life was a mess. His finances were in shambles. Setbacks seemed to seek him out.

Ian had worn himself out looking after his ailing mother during the last year of her life. His wife, whose own family had never been close, couldn't understand why. She turned elsewhere for affection. Soon the marriage was over. The divorce was messy . . . and expensive.

Ian clung to the hope that he could at least be a good father to the teenage children. But then there were problems with drugs and sex. Just the other day someone in the office had overhcard Ian utter the words "probation officer" on the telephone.

Ian's life was falling apart. Now he had turned to alcohol, but only on his own time. It hadn't affected his work. Not yet.

Doreen knew what a great healer Jesus Christ could be. She had become a Christian in her early twenties after a personal crisis pushed her to the edge of despair. At a time when she saw no possibility of love anywhere, a compassionate Christian community had wrapped her in love and given her more support and purpose than she thought possible. Armed with new direction, her life had changed dramatically. She had often shared her new faith with others, but always on her own time and with people who had become close friends. She couldn't stand pushy Christians.

She wondered how she could share her faith with Ian without seeming pushy herself. After all, she was his department head. She held some of the keys to his professional future, and he knew it. She wanted to be sensitive to his needs as well as to her delicate position as his boss.

How would she come across if she became more assertive about spiritual matters? She had never had a personal relationship with Ian. She was many years his elder and had never so much as had a cup of coffee with him outside the work setting.

Wouldn't it seem odd for her suddenly to inject spiritual direction into the relationship? Would she be overstepping her bounds?

No doubt he would be embarrassed to learn that his boss knew the extent of his personal problems. Would he feel obligated to respond affirmatively?

How she wished she had begun earlier to become closer to this hurting young man. Then she would have had a better foundation for intervening now. But she hadn't.

Doreen's own boss was not a Christian. Would he think it improper for her to give spiritual counsel within the company?

Doreen was convinced she had much to offer Ian. She yearned to do so. But how assertively should she share?

Questions to ponder and discuss

1. Missionaries sometimes speak of "rice Christians" who agree to "convert" to gain material benefit. When might people in the workplace be similarly tempted?

2. What experience have you had in giving a forthright Christian testimony without seeming pushy or intrusive? Can witnessing on the job disrupt the workplace atmosphere? Can it be counterproductive?

3. If you owned the company, how would you feel about employees sharing "their gospel" with others on staff? Would it make a difference if the employees were Mormons? If they were Muslims? If they practiced some other religion?

Additional Scripture

See also Ezekiel 3:16-18; Matthew 5:14; James 2:14-17.

3 Truth and References

*Simply let your "Yes" be "Yes," and your "No,"
"No"; anything beyond this comes from the evil
one*

—Matthew 5:37, NIV

THE Bible doesn't say much about job references—or does it? Remember John Mark, the green
recruit (Acts 15:36-39)? Paul wanted to leave him behind; Barnabas said no. Two leaders couldn't agree on
a young man's value, so they parted company. If they
had been asked to write a job reference, their versions
might have been quite different. Later, however,
things must have changed. Paul evidently reconsid-
ered and sent for John Mark "because he is helpful to
me in my ministry" (2 Tim. 4:11).

* * *

Lois didn't like filling out reference forms. Especially this one.

When she accepted a recent promotion, Lois had known it would sometimes involve hard decisions. Now it was hitting close to home.

Beulah, a friend now under her supervision, was a good person who tried hard but was ineffective at her present level of responsibility. The department would function better if she were replaced.

Nevertheless, Lois had hesitated to make any moves. Their families were close. They had been friends and co-workers for a long time.

That was why her heart had raced when she heard that Beulah had applied elsewhere. If she found another job on her own, it would solve a good many problems.

Then Lois got a call from the Apex Corporation personnel manager. He was sending a confidential reference form. He hoped Lois would offer an accurate appraisal of Beulah's performance. Even though he and Lois were competitors, he knew Lois was committed to encouraging her people if they could advance elsewhere.

Lois dreaded filling out that form. She had no difficulty giving Beulah high marks in areas such as "tolerance for persons of other backgrounds" or "harmonious in social relationships with others." But she was going to have trouble with categories like "dependability in completing assigned tasks" and "ability to make responsible decisions." In these areas Beulah was clearly below average.

If Lois answered honestly, Beulah probably wouldn't get the job. That would make Beulah unhappy. And Lois would be stuck with her again. She wasn't sure which concerned her more.

On the other hand, maybe Beulah's lackluster performance was the result of poor training and supervision. Maybe her problems were tied to her current position. Maybe a new job was just what Beulah needed to blossom. *So,* Lois told herself, *if I give her a high rating on this form, my little "fib" might be just what Beulah needs to pull herself together.*

What would be the harm? Personnel directors often took references with a grain of salt. But there was her own reputation to consider, not only as a business executive but also as a Christian in the community. It was her duty to treat Apex Corporation fairly.

Lois studied the other questions on the form. "How would you rate the applicant as a leader and an administrator? Give your general appraisal of the applicant as an employee while working with your firm." Then the kicker: "Our policy is to conduct a telephone follow-up to your written reference." Lois knew it would be easier to leave some things off the written reference, but if there was a telephone follow-up, she'd have to be honest.

She knew it would simplify her life if Beulah got this job. But it would simplify her conscience if she answered honestly.

Lois sighed. She'd answer the easy questions now and leave the hard ones for later.

Questions to ponder and discuss

1. Have you ever faced a similar dilemma in filling out reference forms or if asked to evaluate someone for a job or church agency assignment? What did you do? How did it turn out?

2. If you were in Beulah's position, what would you want your friend to do? Would you want a job for which you might not be properly suited? If judged negatively by a friend, would you accept the evaluation or question the friend's judgment? Should Beulah and Lois have discussed this matter together first?

3. Some firms, fearing legal repercussions, no longer give references, either favorable or otherwise. To what extent should Christians be influenced by society's standards in this area?

Additional Scripture

See also Proverbs 14:25; Romans 3:5-8; Ephesians 4:15.

4 The Pious Pressman

And whatever you do, whether in word or deed,
do it all in the name of the Lord Jesus.
                                        —Colossians 3:17, NIV

T HE following story raises several workplace
issues. A zealous young convert needs help to see
how Monday-to-Friday fits into his larger identity as a
Christian. His intense devotion needs to be seasoned
by a broader outlook that shows work as part of a di-
vine pattern (John 5:17) that matters to God (Eph.
6:7-8).

Perhaps both the young man and his boss could
have their horizons stretched regarding "corporate
sin." God told Moses, "If the whole Israelite community sins unintentionally and does what is forbidden
in any of the Lord's commands, even though the community is unaware of the matter, they are guilty"
(Lev. 4:13).

Then, too, there is the matter of "passing judgment on one another" (Rom. 14:1-13).

*   *   *

For the fifth time that day, Martin got up from his desk. He strode past the typesetting and paste-up departments and pushed through the swinging doors to the new perfector press, which was his pride and joy. He wanted personally to check the register on a big four-color book job. The customer's previous printer had gotten sloppy. Martin, president of Plains Printing, had won a chance to bid by promising high quality.

Martin needed to please this customer. The press had cost a bundle and required a high volume of work to pay for itself. Martin also felt he ought to check on Dennis, the pressman.

Dennis had joined Plains about a year ago. A pleasant young man with a quick wit, he learned fast. When a press job opened up, Martin trained Dennis for the position.

Martin was pleased when Dennis showed interest in spiritual things. He accepted Martin's invitation to attend church with him. Before long Dennis made a commitment to follow Jesus.

Dennis was a zealous convert. Once Martin caught him reading his Bible while the press was running. Martin gently reminded him to keep a close eye on the press. He explained that being a Christian pressman also involved quality control and excellence. Dennis had agreed to save his Bible reading for coffee breaks.

Then Dennis began to fast one day a week. Sometimes that made him light-headed and gave him headaches by mid-afternoon. How, Martin wondered, could he do a good job when not feeling well? One of these days he might hurt himself.

One day Dennis criticized some of the jobs Plains was accepting. He had discussed this with his fellowship group, which felt strongly about social justice issues. First, there was the monthly newsletter of a political action group which Dennis felt was militant. He didn't like being part of the production chain.

Martin cringed. It was a regular printing job with a long and lucrative press run. They always paid promptly.

Then there was the university arts catalog with photographs Dennis found offensive. "This is pretty close to pornography," he complained.

One day Dennis flatly refused to run the press. This time the problem was a publicity brochure for a flashy TV preacher who lived in a mansion and drove a lavish car yet cried out for contributions for the "poor and unsaved."

"I think this guy's a phony," said Dennis.

Martin rued the day he had told Dennis to keep his eye on the press.

Life sure would be simpler around here if Dennis had never become a Christian, Martin grumbled to himself.

One of these days, he thought, he'd have to do something about it.

Questions to ponder and discuss

1. How much responsibility should a Christian employer accept for an employee's spiritual development? Should spiritual disciplines be confined to off-hours?

2. Was Dennis out of line to oppose some materials he was printing? Should the customers' right to "freedom of speech" override his personal convictions?

3. How much moral stake do employees have in the products they help produce or distribute? Does it make a difference if the product is military weapons? Tobacco? Food containing possible safety hazards?

5 A Thumb on the Scale of Justice

*Thieves must give up stealing; rather let them
labor and work honestly with their own hands.*
—Ephesians 4:28

ONE enduring theme of Scripture is compassion for those who need extra help along life's journey. But one person's compassion is another's preferential treatment. This is true in families, in the workplace, and in the judicial system.

Scripture contains numerous illustrations of "preferential treatment," such as the parable of the lost sheep (Matt. 18:12-14), the parable of the workers in the vineyard (Matt. 20:1-16), and the story of the prodigal son (Luke 15:11-32).

For those in positions of power, balancing compassion and fairness can be like walking a tightrope. One has to go ahead in faith, counting it "a very small thing [to be] judged by you or by any human court. It is the Lord who judges me" (1 Cor. 4:3-4).

*   *   *

Sometimes, Ivan thought, the scales of justice needed a little help from the thumb. Like when it came to his expense account.

Ivan felt he'd been unfairly passed over for promotion. He'd invested a lot of time in the company, especially when his children were younger. He had paid his dues and more. He felt he deserved more recognition or perhaps something extra.

That "extra" came on his frequent trips. In some cities he'd stay with friends but charge the firm. He'd take relatives out for luxurious dinners and let the company pay. Once or twice he added an extra leg onto a sales trip so he could visit his daughter at college. He found other ways to divert company money into his own pocket. Since Ivan was trusted, no one ever checked.

Ivan felt the company owed him. At church he looked Evelyn, owner of the firm, straight in the eye without guilt.

Two co-workers were furious when they caught on. Unlike Ivan, they weren't professing Christians. In fact, they resented the religious talk around the office. They felt Ivan in particular was self-righteous. The spiritual tone of the office sometimes made them feel second-class.

When news of Ivan's misdeeds found its way to Evelyn, she was livid. She felt betrayed, not only by a trusted employee but also by a fellow believer who had sat with her on church boards. Moreover, the company's testimony had been compromised and the office atmosphere poisoned.

"My immediate reaction was clear-cut," Evelyn recalls. *"He's got to go. Ivan has to be made an example of.* I felt let down. I thought I'd be perceived as a wimp if I didn't act decisively."

However, when she cooled off, Evelyn used a different approach. After meeting with Ivan, she decided not to fire him even though her best business judgment said otherwise.

"Ivan didn't fully understand why I had passed him over for promotion. In his anger he rationalized his cheating the company. But over the course of our discussions, he was able to see that this wasn't right even under those circumstances," Evelyn says.

Ivan agreed to see a Christian counselor. The subject of restitution came up. Was there a way for Ivan to make up for his stealing?

"I didn't press him," says Evelyn. "I asked him if he wanted to give something back. He did, though we had no way of knowing how much was really involved.

"But that wasn't what I was after. I wanted him back, back at work, and back in the community of believers."

Evelyn's decision to let Ivan keep his job was not without cost. Ivan's effectiveness was severely reduced, because he had lost the respect of several key people in the company. Some staff said Evelyn was making a mistake; Ivan would cheat again. They felt she was giving Ivan preferential treatment. They grumbled about Christians not being fair and "taking care of their own."

Questions to ponder and discuss

1. How widespread is Ivan's kind of behavior? Would it be tolerated in your workplace? Was his offense clear or hard to assess?

2. Ivan didn't confess voluntarily. He needed considerable pressure to recognize his wrongdoing. Would you have given him a second chance? Why or why not?

3. To what extent should church and other religious factors influence such workplace decisions as Evelyn's? Did Ivan's unchurched co-workers have reason to feel second-class? Would Evelyn's or your action be different if Ivan had not been a church member?

6 When You're Offered a Windfall

Whoever walks in integrity walks securely, but whoever follows perverse ways will be found out.
—Proverbs 10:9

GRAHAM Tucker, founder of a workplace chaplaincy in Toronto, has a suggestion for Christian workers. He urges them to conjure up a picture of what the kingdom of God is like, then imagine their workplace as a little corner of that kingdom. How would people treat each other in such a place? How would staff treat clients or customers? How would they treat the competition? What feeling would visitors get as they entered such an office? Would they sense it was a place where Christ reigns?

Many ethical dilemmas become simpler if we realize that when we go to work, we carry God's kingdom with us.

* * *

In their book, *The Power of Ethical Management* (Morrow, 1988), Kenneth Blanchard and Norman Vincent Peale tell a story something like this one.

Competition was fierce and margins were thin. Warren, division sales manager for a large manufacturing company, was feeling pressure to show improvement. He needed new sales blood, someone aggressive, with a lot of experience and savvy.

When Kent walked into his office, Warren thought his prayers had been answered. The man was perfect for the job. He had great sales numbers and knew the industry inside and out after several years with a major competitor. Here was Mr. Right.

However, at the end of the interview, the candidate did something that sucked the wind out of Warren's sails. He reached into his suit pocket and pulled out a small computer diskette. The diskette, he explained, was full of vital data about his previous employer, including customer profiles, marketing strategies, and details of a major contract for which Warren's company was also bidding. Whoever hired Kent would gain a wealth of useful information.

After Kent left, Warren struggled with conflicting emotions. He was infuriated by the blatant offer, as well as chagrined that this excellent candidate turned out to be someone he wouldn't want to work with. He was also painfully aware that he had been offered a windfall. He had no doubt Kent could produce important accounts. He wondered if he could afford to pass up the opportunity.

Complicating the situation was the fact that a top sales executive was ready to retire, creating a vacancy. Warren had given up hope of a promotion because of his division's lagging performance. Some fat new contracts would put him back in the running. With two kids soon to enter college, a move up the ladder would ease his financial pinch.

Warren lay awake that night, listening to voices.

- "Grab this guy before he goes elsewhere. This is a competitive game. We need any edge we can get. After all, business is business."

- "Face it. Someone is going to get this information. Why not you?"

- "Don't be such a puritan. If you overheard some of this information in the locker room at the club, you wouldn't think twice about using it. Just because it's on plastic doesn't make it worse."

- "Not so fast. Do you really want someone like this in your employ? How long would it be until he'd sell *you* down the river?"

Warren was torn. Knowingly gaining from stolen

information offended his sense of ethics. But he was also ambitious. He had to admit he was tempted.

Questions to ponder and discuss

1. To what extent is Warren's dilemma a matter of legality, ethics, or spirituality? How would you help him sort out the different voices he hears? Does Scripture offer clear guidance for a situation like this?

2. Someone has said that "good ethics is good business" and that morality eventually pays off. Do you agree? Does Christian behavior always produce success in the long run?

3. What's harder—knowing the right thing to do, or doing what we know is right? How can Christians gain the strength to do what they know is right?

Additional Scripture

See also Deuteronomy 16:19-20; Isaiah 33:15-16; Matthew 7:15-20; 16:26; Luke 12:15.

7 To Tell the Truth

Anyone, then, who knows the right thing to do and fails to do it, commits sin.

—James 4:17

ONE thing church and corporate editors have in common is the dilemma of deciding how much "truth" to share with readers. Perhaps their best guide in such matters is Scripture, which presents an unvarnished story of candor. We read about a murdering Moses, an adulterous David, a tempted Christ, a denying Peter.

Another issue in the story that follows is that of obedience to authority. The biblical midwives, Shiphrah and Puah, disobeyed orders to kill male babies they delivered (Exod. 1:15-21). Then they lied to their Egyptian superiors—and God blessed them. Their story, while not a parallel to the one that follows, does suggest using our own faith and discretion in deciding such matters.

*   *   *

Amanda's work in the public relations department of a large firm involves writing and editing the
company newsletter, which goes to all employees.
She recently interviewed her chief executive officer
for a message to staff. During the interview the boss
told her, off the record, that there would have to be
layoffs next quarter. But she wasn't to mention it in
her article for fear it would damage morale. Instead,
he told Amanda to include this sentence: "We hope
for steady employment, but our plans are indefinite."

Amanda was downcast as she left his office. She
was being told to tell a lie. What should she do? Go
back and counsel the CEO to be truthful? Do as he
said? Refuse? Look for another job?

She knew this dilemma was familiar to PR workers in business, government, and even the church.
Complete candor didn't always enhance or promote
the image of the firm. She knew that company,
church, and organizational leaders sometimes yield
to temptation to shade the truth about themselves.

Yet she also felt employees had a right to more
accurate information about their own future.
Wouldn't I want some warning of tough times ahead?
she thought. *What if I turned down a new job offer,*

then received a layoff notice a week later? What if I bought a new car or house and suddenly found myself unemployed when the first payment came due?

Amanda argued with herself on the way home from work.

- Technically the CEO isn't lying. He's not promising steady employment but merely saying, "We hope for steady employment."
- Many PR people are seen as "spin doctors," whose task is to present a positive image, not create unrest.
- It's his company, not yours. Your job is to follow orders.
- Go back and argue with the CEO. Persuade him of the error of his ways. Long-term, the damage to morale and the CEO's credibility will be far worse if he lies or gives the wrong impression. How can employees identify with such a shortsighted CEO?

Amanda decided to call an official of the International Association of Business Communicators, which has a code of conduct for PR personnel.

"Counsel the CEO to tell the truth," the official said. "It's your job to know what works and doesn't in the profession. Honesty is the best policy because it works. Explain to the CEO that misleading statements will undermine company credibility, particularly at a time when keeping employee confidence is vital to long-range corporate goals. If that doesn't sway him, then part ways with the company due to irreconcilable differences."

Easy for you to say, Amanda thought. *I can't afford to lose this job.*

Questions to ponder and discuss

1. Should Amanda hesitate to quote the CEO the way he wants? After all, it would be his lie, not hers. Is this any different from a journalist who quotes a politician's campaign promises?

2. If you worked for this company, when would you want to hear about a potential layoff? Do employees have a right to expect forthright and timely information concerning actions that will affect their future?

3. The Bible records the "warts" of God's people, including murder, adultery, deceit, and leaders' quarrels. Should this be a model for Amanda to follow in her work? How about for editors of church periodicals?

8 A Bid Is a Bid

*Suppose one of you wants to build a tower. Will
he not first sit down and estimate the cost to see
if he has enough money to complete it? For if he
lays the foundation and is not able to finish it,
everyone who sees it will ridicule him.*

—Luke 14:28-29

Every parent, teacher, and employer must
sometimes make a choice between compassion and
discipline. It's not always an easy call. Scripture re-
peatedly warns against being "hard-hearted or tight-
fisted" (Deut. 15:7-8) and encourages us to help those
in financial distress (Lev. 25:35-38). But in today's
specialized marketplace, we have also come to see
competent work as part of our Christian witness. It
may seem austere, but Christian love may call us to
help discipline those who are in the wrong line of
work.

* * *

Elmer and his senior managers had spent months planning the new plant addition. Now it was beginning to take shape. Everyone was looking forward to the increased flexibility and volume the addition would bring. Getting over that cramped feeling would be great.

For a time the project had been in question. Last year had been tight. Elmer had toyed with putting the project on hold. Finally he had decided to plunge ahead. "After all," he had told his family, "taking risks is what business is all about."

He had watched with excitement as the excavators moved in and began work. Next came the concrete, and there was plenty of it to be poured. Little did he know the concrete was going to be a big headache.

Well into the job, the concrete subcontractor called to ask for a private meeting. Sam looked visibly shaken as he closed Elmer's office door behind him.

Elmer had known Sam for a long time. Sam's concrete company did good work, though the present job had seemed a bit beyond its scope. When the first bids had come in, Elmer was pleasantly surprised by Sam's competitive quote. In the end, Sam's low bid had carried the day.

"Something wrong, Sam?" Elmer asked now.

"You could say that," Sam said quietly.

He explained that he had just discovered a major blunder in his calculations. A $100,000 blunder. The upshot was that meeting the terms of the contract could jeopardize his company.

Elmer had the figures checked by his own people. They verified the error. Sam's bid had been many thousands of dollars under the next lowest bidder. What to do now? It was too late to switch.

"Shouldn't be our problem," said one of Elmer's executives. "If he hadn't made the mistake, he probably wouldn't have gotten the job in the first place."

"I agree," said another. "He signed it; he should eat it."

Elmer struggled. Should he hold Sam to the terms of the contract? Or should he dig deep to make up for Sam's mistake? That, said his senior financial officer, would be "rewarding incompetence." Moreover, the employees would have to bear part of the brunt of such generosity because the extra $100,000 would affect the company's profit-sharing plan. Was this fair?

Various alternatives were explored. All still seemed to put Sam in financial jeopardy. Amid the protests of his senior staff, Elmer finally decided to pay Sam the overrun.

"We need to live beyond the law, going beyond what is demanded or even expected," Elmer said. "Furthermore, he happens to be a brother in the church. That makes it even more difficult."

Or should it? he wondered.

Questions to ponder and discuss

1. Does the biblical command to "go the second mile" apply in a case like this? Or is Elmer, as one of his executives claims, really rewarding incompetence at the expense of the employee profit-sharing plan?

2. Elmer thinks his dilemma is complicated by the fact that Sam is a brother in the church. Should this make a difference? Should Christians receive preferential treatment in business?

3. What do you think of the comment "He signed it; he should eat it"? Does business normally operate this way? Do consumers operate this way when dealing with manufacturers' warranties?

9 They Call It Harassment

Among you there must not be even a hint of sexual immorality, or of any kind of impurity, . . . because these are improper for God's holy people.

—Ephesians 5:3, NIV

SEXUAL harassment is as old as the Bible. An early incident, with the usual gender roles reversed, can be found in the story of Joseph and Potiphar's wife (Gen. 39). A remarkable feature of the ministry of Jesus is the radical new respect for women.

Evidence includes Luke's honoring of Mary (Luke 1:26-55), new rules on divorce that restrict the power of men (Matt. 19:3-9), a compassionate response to the woman caught in adultery (John 8:1-11), and the fact that Jesus made his first post-resurrection appearance to women (Matt. 28:1-10). This redefined view of women gives some clues as to what Jesus would have thought about sexual harassment.

* * *

Janet, a department manager, was saddened to learn Lucretia was resigning. Lucretia was competent and resourceful. Everyone liked her. She had a good future with the firm.

Then the reason unfolded. Mitchell, single and a rising company star, was paying Lucretia a lot of attention. Too much.

Mitchell was friendly and outgoing, sometimes to excess. Like the time he encouraged a receptionist to stand and turn so he could admire her new outfit. Then he had been transferred to manage a branch in another city. Now he was back at the head office as a vice-president.

He was well-behaved at work, but it was clear he had a special interest in Lucretia. At first it was just the occasional ride home. Lucretia had accepted rides because they lived in the same end of town. Then he asked for a date. He was nice enough, but Lucretia wasn't interested.

Mitchell persisted. He wouldn't leave her alone. Sometimes he'd just show up at places she went. He joined Lucretia's church choir, apparently to be close to her. Once she thought she saw his car parked on her street late at night. Was she being stalked?

Then one day he told her, for no apparent reason, "I'm going to be president of this company. Then you'll want to go out with me."

Janet was shocked. "If that was a threat," she said, "then it's harassment."

Company guidelines described sexual harassment as "unwelcome behavior of a sexual nature or with sexual overtones." There were two different types.

One was "quid pro quo" harassment, whereby decisions affecting employment were based on compliance with sexual requests. The other was "hostile environment harassment." Here unwelcome sexual conduct interferes with a person's job performance or causes an intimidating or offensive work environment.

Janet told Lucretia that the policy also required an investigation of any complaint of harassment or information about suspected harassment.

"No," said Lucretia. She feared that would make things worse.

"Are you afraid for your physical safety?" Janet asked.

Lucretia wasn't sure. There was nothing she could pin down.

"Our policy protects you," Janet protested. She pointed to the last paragraph in the manual. "All reported incidents of sexual harassment will be investigated fully and kept confidential."

"That's easy to say," said Lucretia. "He'd know it was me who reported it. In no time it would be all over church and I'd get branded. Let's just leave this alone. I can find other jobs."

Janet hated to let the matter drop. Should she take action? Or should she respect Lucretia's wishes?

Questions to ponder and discuss

1. Some people would consider this a mild or borderline case of sexual harassment. How much more serious would it have to become for Janet to have no choice but to report it?

2. What obligation does Janet have to future victims whom Mitchell might harass if not confronted now? When does her moral responsibility to foster working relationships of trust take precedence over her desire to respect Lucretia's wishes?

3. How widespread is sexual harassment among Christians? Could Lucretia's situation have occurred in a church agency or a company owned by Christians? Is this an issue for church attention?

10 When Can You Sue?

And whoever does not provide for relatives, and especially for family members, has denied the faith and is worse than an unbeliever.

—1 Timothy 5:8

THE apostle Paul's message on lawsuits (referred to below) seems clear. Yet elsewhere Paul speaks supportively about the governing authorities "established by God" (Rom. 13:1). Presumably these include our current system of laws relating to property, ownership, and bankruptcy.

Is there a time to take advantage of the protection afforded by law? Paul himself used the law (the privileges of his Roman citizenship) to avoid a flogging in Acts 22:22-29. How shall we sort out principles we can rely on today?

* * *

Howard was a young Mennonite in his early twenties. He supported his wife and new baby by working in an agribusiness firm. One day Howard was badly injured in a machinery accident. After a long convalescence, he was left with a significant physical disability and a large cash settlement.

Howard and his wife decided to use much of the cash to build a new house specially tailored to accommodate Howard's permanent disability. As they looked for building sites, they were delighted to learn that a farmer who was a member of their congregation had acreage available along a creek. Unknown to most of the community, the farmer was in serious financial trouble and needed to sell some land to stay afloat.

Howard gladly paid cash for the property. When the house was completed, he and his family had a home that was comfortable but not lavish. By the time he finished paying for it, a good chunk of his cash reserves was gone. Nonetheless, he and his wife felt it was worth it because the special refinements allowed Howard to function as best he could with his disability.

Because Howard had paid in cash, no financial institution was involved in the sale. No one did a title search on the land. Howard himself neglected to do so because, after all, he was buying from a fellow church member. If a search had been done, however, he would have learned that the land was encumbered. In other words, someone else had first rights to the property even though Howard had paid for it.

Unfortunately, things got worse for the farmer. By the time Howard's house was completed, the banks had begun to foreclose on some of the farmer's property (including Howard's house and land).

Howard was beside himself with anger and fear. Where could he turn now? He could no longer provide for his family the way he wanted to before the accident. He and his wife had counted on their paid-up home to let them live on their modest earnings. What would he do now? Rent a small apartment? Then how could he function properly, much less raise a family?

Friends advised Howard to sue. They said he had a good case. At the least he might win back the value of the house.

However, Howard wasn't sure. He had been taught that Christians don't sue one another. Scripture seemed clear on the matter (1 Cor. 6:1-7). His friends, however, said the Bible's words were behind the times. Nowadays, they said, Christians sue all the time.

Questions to ponder and discuss

1. If you were a leader in Howard's congregation, how would you resolve the problem between Howard and the farmer? Or should the church keep out of it and leave the problem for the courts to handle?

2. How would you interpret Howard's dilemma in light of Paul's words in 1 Corinthians 6:1-7? Does Scripture suggest an unrealistic stance?

3. In today's complex business world, it is difficult to keep entirely out of court. From a Christian perspective, are some lawsuits more "acceptable" than others? If so, which ones?

11 More Than Money

Like good stewards of the manifold grace of God, serve one another with whatever gift each of you has received.

—1 Peter 4:10

In his book *Liberating the Laity,* Paul Stevens notes that many churches fail to use the gifts of their laypeople. He describes these as the "frozen assets" of the church. Many churches have lost the art of discerning gifts. Professional ministers increasingly are paid to do the work of ministry.

As a result, highly capable members remain inactive because they are too shy or insecure to try exercising their gifts. Does your congregation coax out and nurture the gifts of its members? Or do you have a vast treasure buried in ice?

* * *

Vic was getting restless. The church business meeting had already gone on for two hours, and Vic had been sitting in what he called a "one-hour chair." But they were nearing the end. It was time for nominations for the annual election of committees.

It took a while to fill the slates for the Christian education, worship planning, and outreach committees. Then came the last one, a new subcommittee of the Board of Trustees that would raise funds for an elevator to make the facilities more accessible for the elderly. The elevator itself wasn't so expensive, but making the necessary modifications to the building would cost $200,000.

Vic squirmed as eyes turned on him. Of course he would be nominated. He was always nominated to every committee that had anything to do with money. As a businessperson, it was expected that his keen sense of financial matters and procedures would be needed.

Vic was always willing to help out. But why did people think his only gift was keeping track of money?

Every year he rehashed the same old arguments in his mind. *I use much more than money in my business. I use material resources, human resources, time, and technology. I don't produce only money. I also produce employment and opportunities for creativity. I know something about focusing activities toward a desired goal. I know how to plan, motivate, correct, and discern abilities and strengths in people.*

He sometimes wondered what would happen if he were put in charge of helping church staff plan ahead for their lives. Could he spend time with young adults who were searching for vocational direction? Could he talk with people who were unhappy in their work and help them understand their abilities as well as their limitations? Could he help other church boards become more innovative in their ministries? Could he offer some fresh insights to the worship planners?

Once or twice he had timidly suggested some of these things, but nothing had developed.

Vic also wondered why no one in church ever asked his opinion about spiritual matters. After all, he had minored in Bible at college. He subscribed to religious periodicals and read several books on theology every year.

The regional manufacturers association frequently asked him to address their meetings, so he couldn't be all that bad as a public speaker. Other lay people got to preach sometimes. Why not him?

Every year Vic pondered all these things. And every year he ended up on the same boards and committees.

He sighed. Any minute now he would be nominated.

Questions to ponder and discuss

1. Is Vic's situation unusual? Are businessfolk in your congregation encouraged to participate beyond a "money" role? If not, why?

2. How far should Vic go in promoting himself for new forms of participation? Should he take the bull by the horns and campaign for a different role?

3. How does your congregation discern the gifts of its members? Does it assume "the cream will rise to the top" or actively find ways for members to expand their involvements?

Additional Scripture

See also 1 Corinthians 12; 7:7; 1 Thessalonians 5:19; 1 Timothy 4:12-14; Romans 12:3-8.

12 When Illness Strikes

How does God's love abide in anyone who has the world's goods and sees a brother or sister in need and yet refuses help?

—1 John 3:17

LOYALTY is a thing of the past in many companies. When people with decades of service are cast aside for the sake of profit or convenience, it's no wonder loyalty is out and cynicism is in. How much loyalty should Christian employers show to their work force?

Should a Christian company be a community where people support and encourage each other, even when they are down? Treating people well only when they are healthy and productive may be similar to what Jesus was talking about when he urged his followers to do more than love those who already loved them (Matt. 5:46-48).

* * *

Roger was coming from the coffeepot with his second morning cup when Nathan passed him in the hallway.

"Morning chief," Nathan said cheerily, unbuttoning his coat.

Roger returned the greeting, resisting the impulse to glance at the clock. *Must be at least an hour late*, he thought.

As he watched his employee put his coat away, Roger sensed that Nathan was unsteadier than usual. Maybe this was one of his bad days. There had been more and more of them.

Even on good days, Nathan wasn't what he had once been, when he was one of the sharpest number-crunchers in town. Then clients jockeyed for his services. He was always on top of changes in tax law and seemed to know instinctively how any new tax interpretation would impact each client's financial picture. In those times, it was a rare day when a tax audit found something amiss in anything Nathan had prepared.

Roger sighed. Those days appeared gone, perhaps forever. Ever since Nathan's illness struck, he'd lost his edge.

In fact, there were days when Roger wondered if Nathan could perform his job at all. The treatments sapped his energy and sometimes seemed to cloud his judgment. When it became obvious that this would be an ongoing problem, Roger had quietly reduced Nathan's load, but even then Nathan made mistakes that could cause tax penalties for clients.

Only last month an error in recaptured depreciation had added a hundred thousand dollars to one company's estimated tax. Fortunately, Roger always had Nathan's work reviewed by others, so the mistake was caught before it caused lasting damage. But double-checking meant extra work for others and a financial drag on the company.

For his part, Nathan was making a monumental effort. A proud man, he showed up—if late—on days when others would have given up. Sometimes he pushed himself too hard. Sadly Roger wondered if the physical strain would eventually shorten the man's life.

There was more than pride at work, however. There was an element of quiet desperation in Nathan's perseverance. He needed the job to get medical insurance and to support his family. His treatments were expensive; he couldn't afford them on his own. Despite his shrewd work with other people's finances, he had never built up much of a cushion himself.

When the illness struck, Roger had vowed to stand by Nathan and be a good Christian brother in his time of need. But, he had to admit, he hadn't really calculated the cost of going the extra mile. Theirs was not a big company. There was a limit to how much charity they could afford without compromising their fiscal health and jeopardizing the jobs of others in the firm.

Roger wondered how far he should go to accommodate Nathan's needs.

Questions to ponder and discuss

1. Should Roger continue to carry Nathan, regardless of the cost to his company? How would you answer if you also worked for this firm and your job security was threatened by Roger's charity? How do you think Nathan would answer?

2. How much responsibility should a Christian employer feel for the health and social needs of employees? Some would argue that such broad concerns might bring us back to a bygone era of corporate paternalism.

3. What does it mean, in today's society, to support fellow workers in a Christian fashion? Is it idolatrous or materialistic to see one's job as a place of Christian community?

Additional Scripture

See also Matthew 5:7; 2 Corinthians 9:10-11; Galatians 6:9-10.

13 The Great Porn Debate

Do not be yoked together with unbelievers. For what do righteousness and wickedness have in common? Or what fellowship can light have with darkness?

—2 Corinthians 6:14-15, NIV

CHRISTIANS have long debated whether it is right to be involved with questionable enterprises in an effort to influence change from within. Scripture seems to give varied signals on the distance we are to maintain from unsavory enterprises.

More clarity is offered on whether the health of a business takes precedence over other moral considerations. When Paul and Silas cast out a demon (Acts 16:16ff.), the formerly possessed woman could no longer make money for her owners. In Acts 19:23ff. the silversmiths complained that Paul was ruining their trade. Perhaps staying in business is not of utmost importance to the biblical writers.

* * *

Some people say he's a pornography peddler. Others say he's an outspoken Christian and active church member. Between those diverse poles lies a large patch of ethical gray.

Rudy talks openly about his faith. He says it "remains an important part of my life today." Some fellow believers were dismayed to learn that his vast business holdings included a magazine distribution company which handles *Playboy* and *Penthouse*. The company distributes thousands of different titles a year, including popular consumer magazines. The adult men's magazines account for one percent of total unit sales.

Some of Rudy's detractors say that since he profits from the offensive magazines, he shares the blame for "this pernicious influence in our midst." Others say his involvement "gives a signal to the rest of society that pornography is acceptable." They don't see how he can be a Christian and distribute obscenity.

Rudy offers his defense.

• It would be difficult selectively to weed out particular periodicals because they come as part of a larger package along with wholesome magazines. Moreover, if he stopped handling the sexually offensive magazines, he would lose business to competitors. "I might as well sell the company and get out of the business."

- Refusing to distribute certain periodicals would be a form of censorship. To discriminate against a sexually offensive magazine, he argues, is to impose his personal views on the public. He points out that he also distributes literature for radical environmentalists and antinuclear extremists, even though he disagrees with their views.

"Once you start discriminating, where do you stop?" By selling all kinds of material, he believes, he is helping preserve freedom of expression.

- He is only one link in a distribution network that includes advertisers, publishers, international distributors, customs officials who let the material into the country, trucking firms, wholesalers, retailers, and customers. No matter what he does, the other links will continue to operate.

- By working within the system, he can help improve it. Selling the company is no solution, he says. "What we need are responsible distributors who care about the community and are prepared to balance freedom of speech with community standards and good taste."

How, his critics ask, is he influencing the magazine distribution business for the good?

Rudy responds that amid a lack of clear government guidelines on what constitutes obscenity, he helped his province set up a review agency. "My reviewers," he explains, "screen the so-called adult magazines. They keep the worst of them off the racks."

One local pastor has said, "Rudy couldn't criticize the business if he weren't in it. He has to take the harder road. If he just opts out, he will lose the ability to help bring about change."

Questions to ponder and discuss

1. Does Rudy seem to be separating his business and his faith into separate compartments? Where else do Christians exhibit the same tendency? What has the church done to help Christians integrate work and faith?

2. Rudy says that if he stopped handling some magazines, he might have to get out of the business altogether. Is this an unacceptable alternative? Why or why not?

3. How valid is the defense that "Rudy couldn't criticize the business if he weren't in it"? In what other kinds of work are we likely to hear the same argument?

Additional Scripture

See also 1 Corinthians 5:9-11; Matthew 9:9-13; Romans 14:1-13.

If you would like
more information on MEDA (Mennonite
Economic Development Associates)
and its various programs
to encourage a Christian witness
in the marketplace,
please call 1-800-665-7026.

The Authors

 **Ben Sprunger** is president of Mennonite Economic Development Associates. MEDA is a 3,000-member organization that promotes a Christian witness in the marketplace and operates development programs in ten countries. He previously operated his own company, Life Skills International, helping public and private agencies develop programs in health, employment, and substance abuse. A former president of Bluffton College, Sprunger has also served as an executive with Quest International, a nonprofit agency specializing in drug and alcohol abuse programs. He and his wife, Sue, have three grown children. They attend Neil Avenue Mennonite Church in Columbus, Ohio.

Carol J. Suter is vice president and legal counsel for MEDA. Prior to joining MEDA in 1995, she was an attorney practicing in Ohio for fourteen years. Her practice focused on handling the management side of employment and labor matters. A former high school teacher, Suter served with MCC for three years in Jamaica. She and her husband, Eugene, are parents of two adult daughters. They live in Kansas City, Missouri, and are members of Rainbow Mennonite Church.

Wally Kroeker has worked in journalism since 1967, primarily in the areas of business and religion. Previously he worked for the *Regina Leader-Post, Winnipeg Tribune, Saskatchewan Business Journal, Moody Monthly*, and the *Christian Leader*. He currently edits *The Marketplace*, a magazine for Christians in business published by MEDA. He and his wife, Millie, have two married sons and a grandchild. They attend River East Mennonite Brethren Church in Winnipeg.